DROUGHT INTERRUPTERS

BREAKING OUT OF A DRY SEASON

SHELIA KING

EDIFYING READS BY MLSTIMPSON ENTERPRISES

CONTENTS

Endorsements	v
Acknowledgments	xi
Foreword	xvii
Introduction	xix
1. The Thirst	1
2. The Drought	9
3. When Did the Drought Start	17
4. The Priority of the Kingdom	21
5. Drought Interrupters	27
6. Unclean Spiritual Forces	47
7. Kingdom Forgiveness	51
8. Kingdom Filled Repentance	57
9. Kingdom Deliverance	61
10. Kingdom Love	65
A Final Note	69
A Prayer to Receive Christ as Lord and Savior	71
References	73
Notes	75

ENDORSEMENTS

I have read many books but never a book on droughts or drought interrupters. I never thought about the possibility that believers could or would have drought interrupters. As I was sitting up in my bed reading this book "Drought Interrupters", the words written moved me to tears as my mind drifted back to several of the drought interrupters I had experienced in my life. But praise God for his mercy and grace to see me through...
Elder Elborah Williams, Grandmothers With Purpose

Shelia speaks the truth that grips your soul. She goes deep, and the words are even richer. This book is a gift in the midst of the struggles and realities of life.
Sharon Harvey, JAM Ministries

This book is made to minister to me and others—GOD wants to deliver and set FREE.
Minister Doris Williams

The Drought Interrupters is a must-read for all ages, men, women, single mothers and young adults that are in a drought and cannot break the cycle. Sheila King is a trailblazer for those of us that are in a drought and looking for a way out. She has provided a step-by-step road map out of a dry season through kingdom principles in Drought Interrupters.

Pastor Emma Davis

Drought Interrupters is a must-read for anyone that is thirsty and in a dry place. In this book, Prophetess Shelia King shares not only her life experiences of being in a dry place, but she provides many tools that will interrupt and help you to overcome your area of drought. Her writing is clear, her focus is on conveying a message, and her aim is to interrupt your Drought.

Minister Mary Hooks

Drought Interrupters is a very thought-provoking, well-written and easy-to-read book for those of us that are thirsty for more of God. It is the answer for understanding the periods of droughts in one's life and how to overcome them.

Elder Cora Brider

The message is very inspirational and you give people hope and faith that no matter what your struggle is, if you trust God he will carry you through.

Lamedra Brooks, Believer

Drought Interrupters is a must-read for all. This powerful, life-changing book enhances understanding on what a drought is, and equips with wisdom and God's Word on what to do during a drought. This book will empower the reader and serve as a valuable reference.

Minister Michelle Stroud

"I knew it was from the Lord, because only He could have come up with a title like that!" Those are the words that made my heart

swell. It just goes to show you from now until the end of time, when Our Lord speaks stop, listen, repeat! There is always that opportunity that you're given to make the choice to listen or not.
Dondra Hayes, Believer

Prophetess Shelia King, Thank you for exposing yourself and allowing us to journey with you as you share this Powerful and timely read. This is a fast moving, Power Packed Word that will encourage believers and attract those seeking encouragement in dry places.
Minister Fran Flowers

Very good and easy read. The writing is very descriptive and flows seamlessly from page to page. The message is very encouraging and gives hope in times of lacking and setbacks.
Noey Santiago, Believer

I love this book, mainly because its not one of those feel good books that oh everything is going to be good at the beginning! True struggles of a new believer and so on! I can pick this book up at anytime and for any struggle or praise I may be going through. Thank you!
Yvonne Stewart, Believer

Copyright © 2017, Shelia King

www.PropheticKingdomIntl.org

All rights reserved. No portion of this publication may be reproduced, stored in a retrieval system, or transmitted in any form or by any means—electronic, mechanical, photocopy, recording, or any other—except for brief quotation in printed reviews, without the prior permission of the author.

Unless otherwise noted, Scriptures are taken from the KING JAMES VERSION (KJV): KING JAMES VERSION, public domain.

Scriptures marked NIV are taken from the NEW INTERNATIONAL VERSION (NIV): Scripture taken from THE HOLY BIBLE, NEW INTERNATIONAL VERSION ®. Copyright© 1973, 1978, 1984, 2011 by Biblica, Inc.TM. Used by permission of Zondervan.

Scriptures marked NKJV are taken from New King James Version® Copyright © 1982 by Thomas Nelson, Inc. Used by permission. All rights reserved.

Scriptures marked ESV are taken from THE HOLY BIBLE ENGLISH STANDRAD VERSION (ESV) Copyright © 2001 by Crossway, a publishing ministry of Good News Publishers. Used by Permission.

All Scripture marked MSG are taken from *THE MESSAGE*, copyright © 1993, 1994, 1995, 1996, 2000, 2001, 2002 by Eugene H. Peterson. Used by permission of NavPress. All rights reserved. Represented by Tyndale House Publishers, Inc.

Published by Edifying Reads, an imprint of MLStimpson Enterprises

P.O. Box 1592

Cedar Hill, TX 75106-1592

Printed in the United States of America

ISBN: 978-1-943563-09-8

Editing by Rose Morgan

Cover by Michelle Stimpson

DEDICATION

To my entire family—both natural and spiritual.
Be encouraged!

ACKNOWLEDGMENTS

First and foremost, I would like to give special thanks to my Lord and Savior Jesus Christ. It has been Your love, saving grace, favor and faithfulness that has allowed me to pen this book. Thank you for always being a Faithful Father, even when I was not!

Special thanks to my pastor and First Lady, Bishop T. D. Jakes and Mrs. Serita Jakes. You both have poured into my life over 19 years and I can truly say that it is because of the love and consistency that you both have demonstrated over the many years that I am the woman of God I am today. Thank you both sincerely!

Also, a special thanks to Pastor Floyd S. Moody and Beverly Moody for your unconditional love and support and for leading me to the Lord. To Bishop Richard Young and First Lady Arlene Young, thank you for teaching me the importance of being filled with the baptism of Holy Spirit and the importance of living a life consecrated unto God. Blessings to you both!

Over the years, there have been many individuals who

have strongly impacted my life and it would take several pages to honor them all. Those relationships and special friendships molded me into the person I am today. God has blessed and favored me by allowing our paths to cross and for that I'm forever grateful!

To my parents, the late Larry Joseph Alexander and Mary Jo Wilson, you both inspired me in too many ways to name. For that I am forever grateful. I love and miss you Dad and Mom!

To my sons and daughters, Larry and Lamedra Brooks and Mikael and Noey Santiago, you all have been there for me through the good times and the challenging times. For that and so much more I'm forever grateful. Blessings!

To my grandchildren: Jasmine, Donny, Nolen, Mason, Julian, Londyn, Jazmine, Jaylen, Larry III, and Janaye and godson Xavier, I pray that this book will inspire you all in your walk with the Lord. With God's grace, mercy, and favor, each of you will grow up to be world changers who will leave a mark in this earth that can never be erased! Blessings!

To my sister, Yvonne Wilson-Stewart, always know that you are so very, very special to me. Thank you for believing in me, for loving me unconditionally, for being my number one supporter of all things. I love and appreciate you, sister, more than you will ever know on this side of heaven.

To my brother, Casey Wilson Sr., thank you for the love that only a little brother can show! You are so very special to me! I love you, sir!

To my cousin, Dondra Hayes, thank you for your love and support throughout the years. You have always been consistent in our relationship. Love you cousin! Blessings!!

Lady Michelle Stimpson, Woman of God, you have been

such a blessing to my life. Thank you for your willingness and sacrifice to help me write this first book. Your patience with me through this entire process has been amazing! Not to mention your beautiful and positive attitude. Girl you ROCK! Thank you for your sincere love and support. I really appreciate you, sister!

To my spiritual mentor, the late Dr. Myles Munroe, thank you for mentoring me from a far. And please know that your practical yet powerful teachings on purpose, leadership, and the Kingdom of God literally changed my life. Dr. Myles, the very significant impact that you made in my life will live on forever! Blessings!

To Arch Bishop Nicholas Duncan Williams, thank you for your powerful teachings on prayer and intercession. These practical truths and spiritual deposits have totally changed how I pray. Thank you, sir, for your sacrifice to nations across this globe!

To Dr. Bill Winston, thank for your teachings on Faith. Your practical teachings on Faith drastically impacted my faith-walk. It was your teachings on faith that caused my faith to catapult to another dimension! Thank you Dr. Winston for living the examples of faith that the entire body of Christ needs to witness! Bless you!

To Apostle Eckhardt, thank you for being obedient to the Lord in having the Writer's Boot Camp earlier this year that I was privileged to attend. I truly believe that because of the meeting in which we received information, revelation, and impartation, I was divinely inspired to complete this book faster than I would have if I had not attended. And I also believe the prophetic impartation that we all received from you was a blessing as well. Again, thank you so very much Apostle Eckhardt! Blessings & Shalom!

To Pastor Valerie Crumpton, thank you for being my best friend, sister, and confidant over the years, and for being that safe place when I needed it most. Love you, sister!

To Elder Elborah Williams, thank you also for our friendship that has been so rich in faith and prayer. Over the years, we have grown to become best friends. You are one that I will forever cherish. Love you!

To Dr. Denise Strickland, thank you so very much for your love, support, and friendship over the years. Also thank you for the sacrifices that you make consistently to help me! You are a tremendous blessing. I'm so very grateful to our Father that HE allowed our paths to cross! Love you!

To Lady Shirley Jackson, thank you for being my friend over the years. Your love and support has meant a lot to me. Bless you Woman of God!

To Pastor Emma Davis, thank you so very much for your love, support and friendship over the years. Woman of God, I have learned so much from you, too much to list. I thank my Lord Jesus Christ for you! Love you dearly!

To Pastor Carl Miller and Cynthia Miller, the both of you have been such a tremendous blessing to my life. Thank you for being there for me over the years when I needed it the most! The impact that you two have made in my life is priceless! Love you both!

To Dr. Linda Morable, Thank you for our very special friendship. You have been a remarkable inspiration to me. And I really appreciate your love and support. Blessings!

To Elder Cora Brider, thank you for being obedient to God in asking me to speak in Lubbock, TX, at the first Drought is Over Conference. And thank you for your faith in God's ability through me to handle the assignment! Bless you, woman of God!

To Elder Prezell McCullough and Janice McCullough, thank you for being great examples of leadership. I really appreciate how you both have demonstrated a love for God's people in your daily walk as sold out believers of Christ.

To Pastor Derrick and Lynnette Alcorn, thank you for the love and support that you have consistently shown towards me through the years. I really appreciate the Godly examples that both have been in word and deed.

To Minister Michele Fullbright, thank you for being a friend and supporter to me. You have been a tremendous blessing in ways too numerous to name. Blessings and Peace be upon you!

To Mr. and Mrs. Hiawatha and Doris Williams, thank you for your love and support and being such a powerful inspiration. And thank you for allowing your light to shine brightly in the market place and in the body of Christ.

To Pastor William and Sonya Purcell, thank you for the love and support that you have shown over the years—and for trusting the God in me to teach God's people. God Bless you both!

To Eder Carrie Livingston, thank you for being a friend and supporter as well as an example of a strong woman of faith and prayer. Always know that the positive impact that you have made in my life will never be forgotten. Bless you woman of God!

To Elder Tiffany Harrison, thank you for our friendship over the years. And for being a powerful example of what it means to be woman of prayer and intercession. I really appreciate you! Blessings & Shalom!

To District Attorney Faith Johnson, thank you for your love and support. And for being such a powerful example of courage, faith and persistence both in the house of God and in the market place! Bless you, Woman of God!

Special thanks to Mother Charlene Nix, Mother Mays and Mother Fran Flowers. You ladies have been such an inspiration in my life. The pearls of wisdom you have shared with me over the years have been priceless! Blessings & peace to you all, true Mothers of Zion.

FOREWORD

Drought Interrupters in many aspects appears to be a transparent look into how the nature of Christ has been formed in the book's author, Sheila King. To the seeker, this clearly written book will inspire an appetite to know the living presence of the Savior. To the believer, it is a powerful handbook which equips and rehearses Kingdom tools given for victorious thoughtful living. It is both valuable and unique as an intellectually accessible yet concise, biblically sound presentation which builds a strong faith foundation.

I commend *Drought Interrupters* to serious readers who crave a convicting truth that will support them through and around seasons of spiritual dryness. I have no doubt that this is the first of a series of works useful in maturing the Body of Christ.

Dr. Cynthia James,
    Associate Pastor of The Potter's House of Dallas

INTRODUCTION

Have you ever experienced a drought in your life and wondered, "Why?" And you pray softly, "Lord, I have tried to live my life in away that's pleasing to you. But I don't see your promises manifesting in my life." You cry out to the Lord in desperation, seeking direction and answers, yet you sense God is not listening. Well, my friend, it is very possible that you are experiencing a drought. And I've come to bring you good news! The purpose of this book is to encourage you and let you know that God is listening and God heard you when you prayed the first word.

First John 5:14-15 reads, "And this is the confidence that we have in him that, if we ask any thing according to his will, he heareth us. And if we know that he hear us, whatsoever we ask, we know that we have the petitions that we desired of him." This promise is for you, too!

This truth was displayed in the Old Testament as well when Daniel, an upright man, prayed fervently for a specific word from the Lord, but the answer to prayer was delayed. Finally, after weeks, an angel came to Daniel. *Then said he unto me, Fear not, Daniel: for from the first day that thou didst set thine heart to understand, and to chasten thyself before thy God, thy words were heard, and I am come for thy words. But the prince of the kingdom of Persia withstood me one and twenty days: but, lo, Michael, one of the chief princes, came to help me; and I remained there with the kings of Persia.* (Daniel 10:12-13)

Friends, I love the story of Daniel because it reminds me of the many times I, too, have cried out to the Lord in desperation when I found myself in situations that were not pleasing to God. It seemed as though the Lord had turned a deaf ear. But in retrospect, I realize He did hear me from the very first day I prayed. Daniel's experience is a great example of how we must continue to believe that the Lord hears our prayers, even though it may appear nothing is happening. I've learned over my life that persistence is the key to breakthrough.

My hope and prayer for you is that this book will encourage and inspire you to know and believe without a doubt: God is listening when you pray. And the very fact you're in a drought is an indication that a part of you is crying out for the One who created you.

In this book, I will share God's proven principles, which I refer to as *Drought Interrupters*. These are very practical, yet powerful keys to receiving relief and victory. If you apply these keys and principles to your life correctly, God's word guarantees you can experience an effective and fruitful life for His glory.

Why Drought Interrupters?

As believers, it is possible to be in drought and not know it. For example, let's say you're at a park in the heat of a Texas summer and you begin to experience an insatiable thirst. Next, you get a headache or maybe even feel nauseous, but you dismiss your body's warning signs because you think to yourself, "It's not that serious. I'll be okay in a minute." You might try to help yourself by wiping off your sweat or taking a sip of a sugary drink, but that doesn't actually help when what you really need is water.

The next thing you know, you are waking up in the local hospital because you did not properly assess and respond to your condition before it got out of hand.

One of the reasons we miss the signs is lack of knowledge. Hosea 4:6 reads, "My people are destroyed for lack of knowledge." The fact is: If your body gets to the point that it activates the demand for more water and you start to feel thirsty, you are already in a state of lack[1]. Ignoring the headaches and nausea that result from dehydration can only make matters worse.

This is the same as being in a spiritual drought and not knowing it. In other words, to me, it's similar to having a limited understanding that the promises of God were ours before the foundation of the world, and because of this ignorance, we quenched our thirst using the world's inadequate ways. Like the person who tries to substitute water with sugary drinks, we rely on our careers or our intellect as our roadmap to success. But God's word advises differently. *Trust in the Lord with all thine heart; and lean not unto thine own understanding. In all thy ways acknowledge him, and he shall direct thy paths.* (Proverbs 3:5-6)

On the flip side, it could be that we are aware of God's word but we choose to ignore what His word declares because we don't recognize the living water flowing in and through us. As a result, we settle for less than God's best. We may see the symptoms of drought played out in our lives when we find ourselves entangled in dysfunctional relationships, or accepting the idea that we can't get out of debt and settling for a life beneath what God intended for us. As royal heirs of God we find ourselves failing to experience life to the fullest.

But thank God, HE is a healer and because of HIS grace, mercy and forgiveness, we no longer have to live our lives in a drought! The Bible is clear that we have a royal inheritance. *In whom also we have obtained an inheritance, being predestinated according to the purpose of him who worketh all things after the counsel of his own will:* (Ephesians 1:11). *For as many of you as have been baptized into Christ have put on Christ. There is neither Jew nor Greek, there is neither bond nor free, there is neither male nor female: for ye are all one in Christ Jesus. And if ye be Christ's, then are ye Abraham's seed, and heirs according to the promise.* (Galatians 3:27-29) We must understand that God never meant for His children to experience a drought in any area of their lives. One of the purposes of this book is to expose the lies of the enemy that keep us from God's perfect will.

1

THE THIRST

This book was birthed out of a series of conferences that took place between 2015-2016. The Lord granted me the privilege of being one of four conference speakers. The meetings were called "The Drought Is Over." All of the speakers had the exciting assignment of sharing this powerful prophetic word in several churches in Lubbock and Arlington, Texas, in Texarkana, and in Arkansas. In these meetings, the momentum built each time we met. We witnessed the supernatural move of God. We saw miracles take place. We saw healings take place, along with individuals receiving deliverance, salvation, and the baptism of the Holy Spirit.

To my surprise, it was toward the end of the conferences when the Lord spoke as clear to me as I know my name. He said: Write a book and call it *Drought Interrupters*. And in it, equip my sons and daughters with principles that will teach them how to interrupt the droughts in their lives.

I knew it was from the Lord, because only HE could have come up with a title like that! Being a native Texan, He knows I'm familiar with blistering days, humid nights, and drought-like weather. When I look back over my life, I see that He has been preparing me for this message all my life. So here we are!

Let me back up and tell you a little about myself. I was reared by my mother, who was a single parent of three children. Our humble beginnings were very loving and nurturing. My father was very much a part of my life but because he was in the military, he traveled quite extensively. He retired from the Air Force as an officer. And although my father wasn't around as much as I would have liked him to be, I still considered him to be my hero. He was a great man of God in my eyes and I learned a lot from him. He taught me the value of working hard and the importance of a disciplined life.

My mother and father were never married, but my mother never spoke negatively about my father. She taught my siblings and I the importance of respecting our father regardless of how we may have felt.

My mother had a relationship with the Lord. She demonstrated her love for the Lord each night as she led my sister, my brother and I in our bedtime prayers. Our mother instilled in us a real love for God and for all people. Mother never met a stranger and I strongly believe her legacy lives on in her children today.

As I grew from childhood into my teenage years, my personal relationship with the Lord began to unfold. I thank God for praying grandmothers because although my mother believed in God, she didn't attend church regularly. Grandmother took us to church and, at the very young ages of nine and ten, my sister and I accepted the Lord Jesus Christ into our hearts as our Savior and Lord. I remember very vividly how she and I would walk through our apartment complex reading our Bibles, and it was then that I knew I wanted to share God's word with everyone I met.

Because of that passion for the Lord and for HIS word, almost immediately I began to experience what I now believe was intense spiritual warfare. I loved the Lord, but suddenly things were beginning to happen in my life that I didn't understand. Add in some of my own typical adolescent rebellion, and I found myself in a wilderness because of disobedience to the word of God. I later came to understand that from the moment I accepted Christ and determined in my heart to share the good news of Christ, the enemy began his evil plot against my life.

The word of God states that "the thief [Satan] cometh not, but for to steal, and to kill, and to destroy: I [Jesus] am come that they might have life, and that they might have it more abundantly." (John 10:10)

Beloved, understand that the enemy feeds off of what you do not know, which is why it is so critically important to know God's word and how to apply the Kingdom principles of God to our everyday life.

Being a young babe in my walk with the Lord, I had no idea of the "life more abundantly" awaiting me on the other side of despair. And little did I know I would experience a drought in my life for several years to come because of my ignorance of what was accomplished at the Cross.

Because my mind was not renewed, my life was still being controlled by my senses—by what I could see, touch, and otherwise experience through my flesh. I was not living life led by the Spirit, as we are told in Galatians 5:16-18: *This I say then, Walk in the Spirit, and ye shall not fulfil the lust of the flesh. For the flesh lusteth against the Spirit, and the Spirit against the flesh: and these are contrary the one to the other: so that ye cannot do the things that ye would. But if ye be led of the Spirit, ye are not under the law.*

Instead, I was living life according to "my way." However, my way was birthed out of ignorance. I didn't know that the decisions I made at the time would have a lasting impact on my life. I didn't realize that following "my way" would catapult me into the worst drought in my life.

In retrospect, I was extremely thirsty for God and I didn't even know it. I was a Christian, but I was unaware of my new identity in Christ. This led to poor decisions as a result of trying to quench this thirst with things other than HIM. And the result of my poor decisions began to manifest the fruit of unforgiveness and fear instead of forgiveness and faith until, finally, I hit rock bottom.

You see, my lifelong dream was to follow in my father's footsteps (remember, he was my hero). My plan was to finish high school, go into the Air Force and begin a career in the military just like he did. However, when I learned I was pregnant in my early teen years, I totally freaked out. I immediately thought my life was over. My next thought was to get an abortion. Although I knew it was not the biblically sound thing to do, the last thing I was thinking about was handling this crisis in a way that was pleasing to God. I tried to justify my decision to have an abortion by reasoning with myself, saying, "First of all, I'm way too young to have a baby. Secondly, who is going to take care of this baby?" To say the least, I was scared out of my mind, not to mention confused and an emotional wreck.

However, there is something about a mother's instinct. My mother knew I was pregnant even before I knew. But she was so distraught of the very idea that it was possible, my aunt was the one that took me to the doctor to confirm my mother's suspicions. And then after it was confirmed, she broke the news to my mother (I didn't have the courage to do it myself because I just knew it would break my mother's heart.)

But my mother's reaction shocked me. Both she and my grandmother emphatically declared there was no way I was going to have an abortion. "You're going to have this baby!"

Although I didn't understand it then, I know now it was the divine providence of God. And I know now that the experience of being a teen mom taught me the importance of responsibility at a very early age. Life as I knew it would never be the same again.

My childhood was over.

But even with this new stage of life, I remained in a drought, unaware of my spiritual condition. There was a thirst in me, but the way I chose to quench that thirst was contrary to the word of God. I was in a place where I thought the best way to quench the thirst was by human means, which resulted in the birth of my second daughter before I finished high school. So there I was, a single teen mother with two children. I didn't know how my life had drifted so far from my goals or that I had played a role in the enemy's plan to keep me from sharing the gospel with people all over the world.

But God! Despite the situation, I *did* know that I wanted a different life; I wanted to experience life abundantly as the scriptures declared. And this was not going to happen unless I really begin to seriously seek the face of God at all costs. My way had failed. Utterly. Now it was time to try God's way.

I later realized that God who is rich in mercy would use every part of this young, scared, confused and broken life of mine for HIS glory. We are assured in Romans 8:28-30 by these words: *And we know that all things work together for good to them that love God, to them who are the called according to his purpose. For whom he did foreknow, he also did predestinate to be conformed to the image of his Son, that he might be the firstborn among many brethren. Moreover whom he did predestinate, them he also called: and whom he called, them he also justified: and whom he justified, them he also glorified.*

Now, please understand that everything in my life was not good, but everything was being *worked out* for good. In other words, what the enemy meant for evil, God used it for my good and for HIS glory.

The word of God says, "Blessed are they which do hunger and thirst after righteousness: for they shall be filled." (Matthew 5:6) The dry place in me stirred up a thirst in me for more of God. The scriptures declare, "Hungry and thirsty, their soul fainted in them. Then they cried unto the Lord in their trouble, and he delivered them out of their distresses. And he led them forth by the right way, that they might go to a city of habitation. Oh that men would praise the Lord for his goodness, and for his wonderful works to the children of men! For he satisfieth the longing soul, and filleth the hungry soul with goodness." (Psalms 107:5-9)

As the hunger and thirst began to be satisfied in my life by seeking God, things began to turnaround. The favor of God began to over take my life. I began a quest to know God on a deeper level and after going through a series of tests, I had the privilege of meeting a very dear friend. I'll call her "Pearl."

Pearl and I worked together back in the nineties. She was such an inspiration to me. Through my friendship with Pearl, I learned the principles of sowing and reaping. While I believe it was a divine encounter to have known Pearl, the Lord knew she had knowledge in areas that I needed to be exposed to desperately. And with that being said, Pearl and I became very, very good friends. I can recall one particular instance where she invited me to her church. There was a revival going on that week. Friends, it was a Holy Ghost set up. All I can say is that my life was forever changed. During this revival, I was filled with the baptism of the Holy Ghost with the evidence of speaking in tongues. When I experienced the power like the Bible speaks of in Acts 1:8, things began to shift supernaturally in my life.

The word of God tells us, "But ye shall receive power, after that the Holy Ghost is come upon you: and ye shall be witnesses unto me both in Jerusalem, and in all Judaea, and in Samaria, and unto the uttermost part of the earth." (Acts 1:8)

The word power in this scripture in the Greek is dunamis (pronounced *doo'-nam-is),* which means ability, abundance, power, strength. This kind of power was what I needed to experience relief from the drought in my life.

Furthermore, it was after being endued with power from on high that I actually experienced and possessed the power of God that Peter talks about in the word of God, the power to live a life victoriously in Christ. Please understand that the tests didn't cease, but with the power came a better understanding of what the enemy was trying to do and how I could resist and overcome his schemes.

Beloved, the word of God instructs, "For the weapons of our warfare are not carnal, but mighty through God to the pulling down of strong holds; Casting down imaginations, and every high thing that exalteth itself against the knowledge of God, and bringing into captivity every thought to the obedience of Christ; And having in a readiness to revenge all disobedience, when your obedience is fulfilled." (2 Corinthians 10:4-6). "And that lest Satan should get an advantage of us: for we are not ignorant of his devices." (2

Corinthians 2:11). These scriptures confirmed that I had the power through Christ.

We need to understand that it is our Father's desire to expose the works of darkness in our lives. We must maintain an advantage over Satan. But understand that this will only come as a result of having a relationship with our Father God.

You may also be asking yourself how this is possible when you never really had a relationship with your earthly father. Well, I'm glad you asked. Please understand that a relationship with God our father was HIS original intent for us from the beginning of time. Yes, it began with Adam. The relationship Adam and Eve had with God in the garden was the ultimate relationship. And in that relationship, God provided everything they would ever need. But unfortunately, the relationship was interrupted because of Adam's disobedience to God (we will talk more about the fall later). The good news is that Jesus came and died and rose again from the dead to restore the relationship back for those who are His.

2

THE DROUGHT

We have already established that it's possible for a believer of Jesus Christ to be in a drought and not even know it. In this chapter, I will cover three very important facts regarding the origin of a drought: What is a drought? What causes a drought? What are the signs of a spiritual drought?

Let's get started.

WHAT IS A DROUGHT?

BELOVED, one of my gifts in the fivefold ministry is that of a teacher. And because of the teacher in me, I dare not assume that everyone knows what a drought is.

This leads me to our first fact. What exactly is a drought?

A Drought is

1. a prolonged period of abnormally low rainfall, leading to a shortage of water.
2. dry spell, dry period, lack of rain, shortage of water
3. a prolonged absence of something specified

Synonyms include: failure, famine, inadequacy, insufficiency, lack, paucity, pinch, poverty, scantiness, scarcity, shortage, undersupply, want, need, absence, deprivation.

Consider our earthly existence. The average adult human body is comprised of 50-65% water. About 71% of the Earth's surface is water covered, and the oceans hold about 96.5 percent of all the Earth's water. Life cannot exist without water. We must constantly be adding fresh water to our body in order to keep it properly hydrated. Water can be a miracle cure for many common ailments such as headaches, fatigue, joint pain, and much more. We can go for weeks without food, but only three days without water![1]

Throughout the Old Testament, there were wars over water wells. *Then Isaac sowed in that land, and received in the same year an hundredfold: and the Lord blessed him. And the man waxed great, and went forward, and grew until he became very great: For he had possession of flocks, and possession of herds, and great store of servants: and the Philistines envied him. For all the wells which his father's servants had digged in the days of Abraham his father, the Philistines had stopped them, and filled them with earth.* (Genesis 26:12-15). *And Isaac digged again the wells of water, which they had digged in the days of Abraham his father; for the Philistines had stopped them after the death of Abraham: and he called their names after the names by which his father had called them.* (Genesis 26:18).

As you can see, water was extremely valuable even in the

biblical days to the extent that individuals lost their lives in an attempt to maintain and/or possess their water rights.

But the Word promises, *Therefore with joy shall ye draw water out of the wells of salvation. And in that day shall ye say, Praise the Lord, call upon his name, declare his doings among the people, make mention that his name is exalted. Sing unto the Lord; for he hath done excellent things: this is known in all the earth. Cry out and shout, thou inhabitant of Zion: for great is the Holy One of Israel in the midst of thee.* (Isaiah 12:3-6)

Be encouraged! The Lord is saying for everywhere the enemy has stopped your wells, HE will unstop them. With joy shall you draw water of God's wells of salvation!

And it shall be, when the Lord thy God shall have brought thee into the land which he sware unto thy fathers, to Abraham, to Isaac, and to Jacob, to give thee great and goodly cities, which thou buildedst not, And houses full of all good things, which thou filledst not, and wells digged, which thou diggedst not, vineyards and olive trees, which thou plantedst not; when thou shalt have eaten and be full; (Deuteronomy 6:10-11)

You must believe by faith that what the Lord has for you is for you, and there is nothing anyone can do about it. Understand that God set things in motion to bless you before you were even born. *For I know the thoughts that I think toward you, saith the Lord, thoughts of peace, and not of evil, to give you an expected end.* (Jeremiah 29:11)

It is so.

There is a thirst that only Jesus can satisfy. Problems, issues and circumstances often cause a "thirst" for a solution, but we need to reject temporary fixes for life's difficulties. For instance, you lose your job, but instead of seeking God for direction for what's next in your life, you turn to drugs or alcohol to try to self-medicate the feelings of uncertainty about how you are going to pay your bills and feed your family now. Or your spouse works a lot of hours and has made his responsibilities at the job a priority over you and the kids. But instead of going to God for a solution to this fixable problem, you file for a divorce.

You are not the first person to find yourself in a painful situation. *Jesus answered and said unto her, Whosoever drinketh of this water shall thirst again: But whosoever drinketh of the water that I shall give him shall never thirst; but the water that I shall give him shall be in him a well of water springing up into everlasting life. The woman saith unto him, Sir, give me this water, that I thirst not, neither come hither to draw.* (John 4:13-15) There is a remedy in HIM.

What causes a drought?

A DROUGHT CAN BE a result of any number of things, but for the purposes of this book, I have come to realize that a drought can be the result of a lack of intimacy with the Lord. When God is not a priority in your life, it's reflected in your spiritual life, finances and in your relationships.

Putting God first is more than lip service. *These people draw near to Me with their mouth, And honor Me with their lips, But their heart is far from Me"* (Matthew 15:8). There are times when you say God is a priority in my finances and you know you should be giving God a tenth of your gross income but instead, when you get paid, you pay everyone else, and give God what's left. That's not putting God first in your finances.

Or you say, "Lord I'm going to make you a priority as I start my day every morning by committing time for devotion." But instead, you sleep until the last minute and rush out of the door, because you don't have time to spend with the Lord.

The lack of intimacy with the Lord ultimately will start to manifest drought-like characteristics in every area of your life. Therefore beloved, we must make God a priority. "But seek ye first the kingdom of God, and his righteousness; and all these things shall be added unto you." (Matthew 6:33)

When I began to really make God a priority in my life, things began to drastically turnaround. I began to see God's grace and favor on my life. The desire for prayer and fellowship with the Lord begins to intensify. I begin to receive promotion both spiritually and in the marketplace. The Lord taught me HIS Kingdom principles that related to money, and as I began to operate in those principles, the Lord gave me wisdom and a strategy to get out of debt.

As I began to make the Lord a priority, the Lord allowed me to develop fruitful relationships. I began to learn the difference between fruitful and unfruitful connections.

These are just a few of the many benefits that can be yours as you decide today to make the Lord a priority in your life.

What are signs of a spiritual drought?

UNTIL WE LEARN in God's word what life is supposed to be like, we will unfortunately settle for less than God's best. In other words, as believers, our mindset should be that we are more than conquerors in Christ Jesus. We are above and not beneath. We are victorious in HIM.

When we stop and reflect over our lives, can we really be honest and truly say we clearly see the drought in our lives? I can tell you from experience that until I began to come into the knowledge of who God was and is—only then could I recognize the signs of a drought in my life. Coming into the knowledge of God caused me to realize that I was living beneath my privileges as a Kingdom citizen. All of a sudden, I was able to pinpoint the things that were out of line with what God called me, and the clear evidence of a drought stood out like glaring, neon signs.

One clear signal for me was a lack of peace. I was constantly in a state of unrest. This was primarily because of my poor choices in male relationships. I didn't know what a godly relationship looked like. And as a result, my choice in relationships were clearly less than God's best. My relationships were very unfruitful and left me feeling void and empty. Later down the road, as I began to understand God's word, I recognized this as a sign of drought.

Another sign was lack and debt. I was caught up in a cycle and had no clear path of escape. These scriptures showed me God's heart toward me in this area: 1) *Beloved, I wish above all things that thou mayest prosper and be in health, even as thy soul prospereth.* (3 John 1:2). *Let them shout for joy, and be glad, that favour my righteous cause: yea, let them say continually, Let the Lord be magnified, which hath pleasure in the prosperity of his servant.* (Psalms 35:27).

Beloved, when we talk about a drought, it also means a dry place, and I'm reminded of the words in Matthew 12:43-45 (NKJV). "When an unclean spirit goes out of a man, he goes through dry places, seeking rest, and finds none. Then he says, 'I will return to my house from which I came.' And when he comes, he finds it empty, swept, and put in order. Then he goes and takes with him seven other spirits more wicked than himself, and they enter and dwell there; and the last state of that man is worse than the first. So shall it also be with this wicked generation."

As believers, once we have been delivered, we cannot

leave the spiritual rooms in our lives empty. We have a responsibility with God's help to saturate our lives with washing of our minds with God's word daily. And make sure our spiritual rooms are filled with worship, praise, prayer and God's word.

Decree and Declare, NO MORE DRY PLACES!!

A drought can manifest in the following ways. Here are some of the blatant, tell-tale signs along with scriptures on which to meditate and apply in your life, for the word of life-giving water!

1. Lack of Passion for His Word

It is written: 'Man shall not live on bread alone, but on every word that comes from the mouth of God.' " (Matthew 4:4 NIV)

2. Lack of Prayer –

"Rejoice evermore. Pray without ceasing." (1 Thessalonians 5:16-17)

3. Lack of Peace

"Finally, brethren, farewell. Be perfect, be of good comfort, be of one mind, live in peace; and the God of love and peace shall be with you." (2 Corinthians 13:11)

"Follow peace with all men, and holiness, without which no man shall see the Lord:" (Hebrews 12:14)

Jesus - says - "Peace I leave with you, my peace I give unto you: not as the world giveth, give I unto you. Let not your heart be troubled, neither let it be afraid." (John 14:27)

4. Lack of Purpose (When you don't understand the purpose for which you were created, you will continue to encounter confusion in your life.)

"There is a way which seemeth right unto a man, but the end thereof are the ways of death." (Proverbs 14:12)

"The Lord hath made all things for himself: yea, even the wicked for the day of evil." (Proverbs 16:4)

"A man's heart deviseth his way: but the Lord directeth his steps." (Proverbs 16:9)

"Many are the plans in a person's heart, but it is the Lord's purpose that prevails." (Proverbs 19:21 NIV)

5. Lack of God's Prosperity

"The blessing of the Lord, it maketh rich, and he addeth no sorrow with it." (Proverbs 10:22)

"There is that scattereth, and yet increaseth; and there is that withholdeth more than is meet, but it tendeth to poverty. The liberal soul shall be made fat: and he that watereth shall be watered also himself." (Proverbs 11:24-25)

"He that trusteth in his riches shall fall: but the righteous shall flourish as a branch." (Proverbs 11:28)

"Beloved, I wish above all things that thou mayest prosper and be in health, even as thy soul prospereth." (3 John 1:2).

The list above is of course in no way exhaustive. I've only attempted to list a few of the ones that I have encountered. These were manifested deficits in my life that did not mirror God's promises for my life. Therefore my hope for you is that you begin to seek God in earnest, and if there is any area in your life that is not fruitful, that it is exposed. My desire is that you will begin to decree and declare supernatural change and deliverance over those areas in Jesus' name. Amen!

3

WHEN DID THE DROUGHT START

If you want to know the origin of a thing, you always want to go to the book of beginnings. And yes, I'm referring to the book of Genesis.

There is always a cause and effect. And we see this all through the word of God.

Before Adam was placed in the garden, there was not a shortage of water. God supplied him with everything he would need. At the time GOD made Earth and Heaven, before any grasses or shrubs had sprouted from the ground — GOD hadn't yet sent rain on Earth, nor was there anyone around to work the ground (the whole Earth was watered by underground springs)—GOD formed Man out of dirt from the ground and blew into his nostrils the breath of life. The Man came alive—a living soul! (Genesis 2:5-7 MSG)

A river flows out of Eden to water the garden and from there divides into four rivers. The first is named Pishon; it flows through Havilah where there is gold. The gold of this land is good. The land is also known for a sweet-scented resin and the onyx stone. The second river is named Gihon; it flows through the land of Cush. The third river is named

Hiddekel and flows east of Assyria. The fourth river is the Euphrates. (Genesis 2:10-14 MSG)

There was not a drought in the Garden of Eden. As a matter of fact, Adam had it made before he was even placed in the garden.

The Lord God took the man and put him in the Garden of Eden to work it and take care of it. And the Lord God commanded the man, "You are free to eat from any tree in the garden; but you must not eat from the tree of the knowledge of good and evil, for when you eat from it you will certainly die." (Genesis 2:15-17 NIV)

Clearly, something happened to mess up Adam's paradise. There was a cause and effect. We refer to this chain of events as "the fall". During the fall, Adam gave his authority in the earth to satan. Adam lost his dominion to rule in the earth. And as a result, sin entered into the earth. Because of the Adam's dreadful decision to disobey God, things become very difficult for Adam and Eve.

God told Adam: "Because you listened to your wife and ate from the tree That I commanded you not to eat from, 'Don't eat from this tree,' The very ground is cursed because of you; getting food from the ground Will be as painful as having babies is for your wife; you'll be working in pain all your life long. The ground will sprout thorns and weeds, you'll get your food the hard way, Planting and tilling and harvesting, sweating in the fields from dawn to dusk, Until you return to that ground yourself, dead and buried; you started out as dirt, you'll end up dirt." (Genesis 3:17-19 MSG)

The fall of man from dominion resulted in the ground being cursed and a drought in the Earth. Adam committed high treason, which is the crime of betraying one's country, especially by attempting to kill the sovereign or overthrow the government.

This was the beginning of satan's government system being released in the earth, also known as the kingdom of darkness. But I've got good news. We are a part of another government—the government of the Kingdom of God.

The word says, "For to us a child is born, to us a son is given, and the government will be on his shoulders. And he will be called Wonderful Counselor, Mighty God, Everlasting Father, Prince of Peace. Of the greatness of his government and peace there will be no end. He will reign on David's throne and over his kingdom, establishing and upholding it with justice and righteousness from that time on and forever. The zeal of the Lord Almighty will accomplish this." (Isaiah 9:6-7 NIV) We were redeemed by one man's obedience. Jesus was born to die as the ultimate sacrifice necessary to redeem mankind back unto Himself. He died on the cross and on the third day rose from the grave with ALL power, ALL authority and ALL dominion. He took the keys of death, hell and the grave. Hallelujah.

We understand that by one man's disobedience (Adam) a curse was released. But by one man, Jesus, the Abrahamic covenant blessing was restored!

Disobedience releases a drought. Obedience interrupts the drought, whether spiritual or natural.

Remember, it will take obedience and a hunger for more of God to release the rain. *For I will pour water upon him that is thirsty, and floods upon the dry ground: I will pour my spirit upon thy seed, and my blessing upon thine offspring: And they shall spring up as among the grass, as willows by the water courses.* (Isaiah 44:3-4)

The Bible says in Isaiah 1:19 -20, "If ye be willing and obedient, ye shall eat the good of the land: But if ye refuse and rebel, ye shall be devoured with the sword: for the mouth of the Lord hath spoken it."

The NET version of that scripture reads, "If you have a willing attitude and obey, then you will again eat the good crops of the land. But if you refuse and rebel, you will be devoured by the sword. Know for certain that the LORD has spoken."

I'm sure there have been many times that the Lord told us to do one thing and we did the opposite. I know I can remember several instances when I was a "babe" in Christ and the Lord gave me specific instructions, but I flat out disobeyed Him. That disobedience cost me several laps around the same mountain.

4

THE PRIORITY OF THE KINGDOM

The Lord often speaks to me in illustrated sermons. One in particular comes to mind regarding the time when I was in Cleveland, Ohio for business. Normally, when I pick up a rental car, I make sure that I obtain a toll pass in the event the route that I have to travel for court has toll roads.

Well, wouldn't you know on this particular trip I forgot to request a toll pass from the attendant. On my way to court in the morning, I knew that if I stopped to pay the toll fee, it would certainly slow me down. So I began to calculate in the GPS how long it would take me to get to the destination if I avoided the toll road route. I set the GPS to avoid tolls. What I didn't realize was that, although I would avoid the toll roads, the route would add an extra twenty minutes to my trip.

Yes, you guessed it—I paid the toll and took the shorter route. The Lord immediately spoke to me: *That's what the body of Christ does*. They often look for shortcuts to obtain the Anointing not realizing that there are no short cuts without paying a cost. This cost consists of a lot of studying, fasting and seeking God's face. All of this results in a very disciplined life, which really helped me to develop a more serious and meaningful relationship with God. To possess the anointing of God, we must be willing to live a sacrificial and consecrated life or run the risk of taking the long route and be late for our God-given assignments.

What I'm saying, beloved, is that if you choose to disobey God, it can and will release a drought in your life.

The Kingdom of God must be a priority.

Wherefore, if God so clothe the grass of the field, which to day is, and to morrow is cast into the oven, shall he not much more clothe you, O ye of little faith? Therefore take no thought, saying, What shall we eat? or, What shall we drink? or, Wherewithal shall we be clothed? (For after all these things do the Gentiles seek:) for your heavenly Father knoweth that ye have need of all these things. But seek ye first the kingdom of God, and his righteousness; and all these things shall be added unto you. (Matthew 6:30-33)

We must also understand that God has a benefits package available for us if we choose to obey Him. But know it is a choice that we all must make.

And it shall come to pass, if thou shalt hearken diligently unto the voice of the Lord thy God, to observe and to do all his commandments which I command thee this day, that the Lord thy God will set thee on high above all nations of the earth: And all these blessings shall come on thee, and overtake thee, if thou shalt hearken unto the voice of the Lord thy God. Blessed shalt thou be in the city, and blessed shalt thou be in the field. Blessed shall be the fruit of thy body, and the fruit of thy ground, and the fruit of thy cattle, the increase of thy kine, and the flocks of thy sheep. Blessed shall be thy basket and thy store. Blessed shalt thou be when thou comest in, and blessed shalt thou be when thou goest out. (Deuteronomy 28:1-6)

The Prophet Elijah lived a life that reflected the Kingdom of God as a priority. And because of the sacrificial life that he lived, I believe the Lord knew that He could trust him with great power and authority to be able to represent the Kingdom of God well.

In 1 Kings 17, the Lord used the prophet Elijah to predict a drought because of years and years of disobedience of a long lineage of evil Kings.

Now Elijah the Tishbite, of Tishbe in Gilead, said to Ahab, "As the Lord, the God of Israel, lives, before whom I stand, there shall be neither dew nor rain these years, except by my word." (1 Kings 17:1 ESV). The drought lasted for three years.

Who was Elijah? Well, the name Elijah (in its fuller and more sonorous Hebrew form, Elijahu) means "Jehovah is my God." Elijah's lineage is entirely unknown. So completely are all previous traces of Elijah lost in mystery that Talmudic legends confused him with Phineas, the son of Aaron, the avenging and fiercely zealous priest; and even identified Elijah with the angel or messenger of Jehovah who appeared to Gideon and ascended in the altar flame.

While we know that Elijah was a great prophet who was used mightily by God, he also had some insecurities. In 1 King 18, he defeated the prophets of Baal on Mount Carmel, yet he ran from a threat spoken by Jezebel.

Also notice that Elijah wasn't affected by the drought. He was still performing miracles during the three and half year drought. This is not surprising because *Blessed is the man that trusteth in the Lord, and whose hope the Lord is. For he shall be as a tree planted by the waters, and that spreadeth out her roots by the river, and shall not see when heat cometh, but her leaf shall be green; and shall not be careful in the year of drought, neither shall cease from yielding fruit.* (Jeremiah 17:7-8)

This leads me to my next point: You can flourish in a drought if you would just trust and believe God right where you are! We also must be honest with ourselves and understand that if we are not flourishing in every area of our lives, we need to seek God and find out why. And I thank God that He will not leave us ignorant of the enemy's devices.

Beloved, I would like to share another account in the word of God demonstrating how it pays to obey God.

In I King 17-7-16, we meet Elijah and the Widow at Zarephath. During the time of the drought, she obeyed the prophet:

The Prophet asked would you bring me a little water in a jar so I may have a drink?" As she was going to get it, he called, "And bring me, please, a piece of bread.

For this is what the Lord, the God of Israel, says: 'The jar of flour will not be used up and the jug of oil will not run dry until the day the Lord sends rain on the land.'" She went away and did as Elijah had told her. So there was food every day for Elijah and for the woman and her family. For the jar of flour was not used up and the jug of oil did not run dry, in keeping with the word of the Lord spoken by Elijah. (1 Kings 17:7-16 NIV)

Please note: It was first, Elijah's obedience to God! And then secondly, the widow woman's obedience to the Prophet. It's amazing how simple obedience to God will allow you to prosper in the midst of a drought! Simply a cause and effect.

We must understand that every promise you receive from the Lord, you will receive by faith. And if God said it, that settles it. We see our example of this principle in 1 King 18:42-46.

Ahab went up to eat and to drink. And Elijah went up to the top of Carmel; and he cast himself down upon the earth, and put his face between his knees,

And said to his servant, Go up now, look toward the sea. And he went up, and looked, and said, There is nothing. And he said, Go again seven times. And it came to pass at the seventh time, that he said, Behold, there ariseth a little cloud out of the sea, like a man's hand. And he said, Go up, say unto Ahab, Prepare thy chariot, and get thee down, that the rain stop thee not. And it came to pass in the mean while, that the heaven was black with clouds and wind, and there was a great rain. And Ahab rode, and went to Jezreel. And the hand of the Lord was on Elijah; and he girded up his loins, and ran before Ahab to the entrance of Jezreel.

The prophet made a declaration that the drought was over. And although it hadn't rained in three and a half years at his word, the Lord told him to go to King Ahab and declare that the drought was over. Now, please know that this was no easy task for Elijah. Yet, the prophet knew he had to obey God.

Elijah exercised his Kingdom authority when he told King Ahab the drought was over!

Like Elijah, we have been given dominion as Kingdom Citizens and Kingdom Ambassadors! Therefore, we must exercise our legal rights in the earth. We have had rights from the first day. *And God said, Let us make man in our image, after our likeness: and let them have dominion over the fish of the sea, and over the fowl of the air, and over the cattle, and over all the earth, and over every creeping thing that creepeth upon the earth.* (Genesis 1:26)

The Hebrew word for dominion is râdâh (pronounced *raw-daw'*). It means to *tread* down, that is, *subjugate*; specifically to *crumble* off: - (come to, make to) have dominion, prevail against, reign, (bear, make to) rule, (-r, over), take.

By Psalm 115:16, we know that we are to rule over the

earth: *The heaven, even the heavens, are the Lord's: but the earth hath he given to the children of men.*

In the words of our brother in Christ, Dr. Bill Winston, "The Kingdom of God must be demonstrated. The word of God was never meant to be dictated, but demonstrated."

5

DROUGHT INTERRUPTERS

In this chapter I would like share what I call drought Interrupters. These practical Kingdom Keys or principles will interrupt the drought in your life, if applied. Please understand that keys are necessary to unlock supernatural doors that you otherwise wouldn't have been able to unlock. In other words, when you have access, you no longer have to knock to gain access.

In Matthew 16:19, Jesus said, "And I will give unto thee the keys of the kingdom of heaven: and whatsoever thou shalt bind on earth shall be bound in heaven: and whatsoever thou shalt loose on earth shall be loosed in heaven."

The exciting, essential component of Drought Interrupters that you must have is faith in God. This is absolutely necessary if you are to begin to see manifestations of these Kingdom Keys at work in your life.

The second requirement is that you must be faithful and obedient to God and His word. As long as you continue in your own reasoning, following your own self-made path, your faith has no truth to stand on. Faith in you, faith in your unrenewed mind, faith in the ways of this world will only lead to more disappointment.

You must be thirsty, for the word of God declares, "For I will pour water upon him that is thirsty, and floods upon the dry ground: I will pour my spirit upon thy seed, and my blessing upon thine offspring: And they shall spring up as among the grass, as willows by the water courses." (Isaiah 44:3-4)

Here are some Kingdom Keys to break through a drought.

Drought Interrupter #1: Kingdom Fellowship with God in prayer

Archbishop Nicholas Duncan Williams says it this way, "Prayer is a daily necessity for daily triumph."

For we have not a high priest which cannot be touched with the feeling of our infirmities; but was in all points tempted like as we are, yet without sin. Let us therefore come boldly unto the throne of grace, that we may obtain mercy, and find grace to help in time of need. (Hebrews 4:15-16)

As we journey through this thing called life, I believe that from the beginning of time God pre-wired all of human kind to possess a void inside that only He could fill. Oftentimes we look to religion, careers, relationships and sometimes drugs and alcohol to fill the void. The harsh reality is that none of those things can fill the void permanently. They can only distract us from the void. It's only when you cultivate intimacy with your creator through prayer that you find your purpose.

You may be asking, "Does God really answer prayers?"

The answer is, "Yes." When we talk to God, it's not about praying a certain way or using a certain formula. The reality is, God looks at your heart. There may be times when you're facing a crisis. Life has thrown you a curveball and you cannot find any words in the English vocabulary to speak.

In times like these, the only words you can muster are, "Jesus, I need you right now." This heartfelt prayer will be heard by our loving Father.

If you struggle with the do's and don'ts of prayer, you are not alone. The disciples (who were actually in the physical presence of Jesus) had some concerns about how to pray, too. They asked, "Lord teach us how to pray."

And it came to pass, that, as he was praying in a certain place, when he ceased, one of his disciples said unto him, Lord, teach us to pray, as John also taught his disciples. And he said unto them, when ye pray, say, Our Father which art in heaven, Hallowed be thy name. Thy kingdom come. Thy will be done, as in heaven, so in earth. Give us day by day our daily bread. And forgive us our sins; for we also forgive every one that is indebted to us. And lead us not into temptation; but deliver us from evil. (Luke 11:1-4)

All through scripture we are encouraged to pray:

- *And he spoke a parable unto them to this end, that men ought always to pray, and not to faint;* (Luke 18:1)
- *and Pray without ceasing. In every thing give thanks: for this is the will of God in Christ Jesus concerning you.* (1 Thessalonians 5:17-18).

The power of prayer is the secret weapon for victory for all believers. It is a privilege to be able to go to God in prayer and to be confident in knowing that HE hears us when we pray. *Call unto me, and I will answer thee, and shew thee great and mighty things, which thou knowest not.* (Jeremiah 33:3)

There are so many benefits when we pray, one of which is an opportunity to spend time with God. Getting to know HIM is a reward within itself. Knowing HIM as Father, Comforter, Advisor, Defender, Protector...I could go on and on. We all know life can get lonely, scary, confusing, and disappointing. Knowing your Daddy makes everything all right even when everything seems all wrong.

Also, prayer brings an opportunity to build up your spirit man. *These be they who separate themselves, sensual, having not the Spirit. But ye, beloved, building up yourselves on your most holy faith, praying in the Holy Ghost,* (Jude 1:19-20.

Finally, I mentioned that when we pray, we must be confident in the fact that God hears us. But we also must understand that when we don't see the manifestation of what we have prayed for right away, it still means God heard. That's why our Bible tells us, "and all things, whatsoever ye shall ask in prayer, believing, ye shall receive." (Matthew 21:22) Prayer is how we illustrate God's power at work with us. To quote John Wesley, "Without God man cannot. But without Man God will not!"

Drought Interrupter #2: Live by Kingdom Faith

Everything in the Kingdom is activated by faith. Hebrews 11:1 gives us the very definition of faith. *Now faith is the substance of things hoped for the evidence of things not seen.* Faith is *now*, not *will be*. In other words, your healing is *now*. Your breakthrough is *now*. Your deliverance is *now*, not *it's going to be*. Faith is not dictated by time. Beloved, understand that whatever trial or test you may be experiencing, faith is the legal tender that will release what is yours in the spirit and bring it forth in the natural.

Faith is a fruit of the spirit. *But the fruit of the Spirit is love, joy, peace, longsuffering, gentleness, goodness, faith, meekness, temperance: against such there is no law.* (Galatians 5:22-23) When you became born again, you were given the seed of faith. In fact, we have this promise in scripture, too. *For I say, through the grace given unto me, to every man that is among you, not to think of himself more highly than he ought to think; but to think soberly, according as God hath dealt to every man the measure of faith.* (Romans 12:3) The measure of faith must be exercised in order for it to grow. *So then faith cometh by hearing, and hearing by the word of God.* (Romans 10:17)

You can exercise and grow your faith by hearing the Word on CD, or by watching a worship service that is sharing the word of God. But don't just watch. You must say the word out loud so that you may hear it in order for your faith to grow.

I also believe that you hear the word of God with your spiritual ear. So in the event you are currently deaf or hard of hearing in the natural, you are not left out.

Personally, I watch Bishop T.D. Jakes, Dr. Myles Munroe, Dr. Bill Winston or Arch Bishop Duncan Williams on YouTube, frequently. Over the years, as I've listened to these mighty men of God speak His word, my life changed drastically. Hearing the word preached has grown my faith, my character and my direct relationship with God.

Faith must be a lifestyle. Faith is not something we can play around with casually. *Now the just shall live by faith: but if any man draw back, my soul shall have no pleasure in him.* (Hebrews 10:38) We oftentimes say, "Lord I want to please you." Well, living by faith is a very practical way to please HIM.

By faith Enoch was translated that he should not see death; and was not found, because God had translated him: for before his translation he had this testimony, that he pleased God. But without faith it is impossible to please him: for he that cometh to God must believe that he is, and that he is a rewarder of them that diligently seek him. (Hebrews 11:5-6)

We must also be careful as we are operating in this second drought interrupter that our faith is in the correct thing. Although we all know that education is important, we cannot put faith in our degrees. Relationships with spouses are important, but we cannot put our faith in a spouse (or any human being, for that matter). Our faith should be in God alone. *And in the morning, as they passed by, they saw the fig tree dried up from the roots. And Peter calling to remembrance saith unto him, Master, behold, the fig tree which thou cursed is withered away. And Jesus answering saith unto them, Have FAITH in God.* (Mark 11:20-22) Jesus was telling them to have the "God" kind of Faith.

When our faith is being tested (and believe me when I tell you it will be tested!), the word of God tells us to put our trust in God and God alone. When you place your trust in HIM, you will come out on the other side victorious.

I remember having a desire to be totally out of debt. I began to seek God for a strategy, and He began to challenge me in the area of giving. In 2 Corinthians 9:6, we are given this principle, "But this I say, He who sows sparingly will also reap sparingly, and he who sows bountifully will also reap bountifully". So as I took a leap of faith and sowed a significant seed in faith, things began to turnaround in my finances. I started receiving several paid speaking engagements. There was a spiritual release in my prayer life. I felt like I was able to pray with more power and effectiveness. And I believe this was all a result of my obedience to God in the area of giving financially.

DROUGHT INTERRUPTER #3: Kingdom-Filled Positive Words

YOU MUST ONLY SAY what God says, not what you see. This world is moved by what it sees. And oftentimes what we see is contrary to what we know God's word says. For instance, you are a single parent and you may be experiencing a drought in your finances and feel you're working a dead-end job with no possibility of increase or promotion.

But the word tells us that God call things that be not as though they were (Romans 4:17). As imitators of HIM, we should do the same. Oftentimes, that's easier said than done, and that's because we have been conditioned to be led by our senses and not by faith.

Let me share some samples that may help you understand this concept of filling your mouth and your life with positive, God-based words:

Don't say: I'm sick in my body.

Say: With His stripes, I'm healed. (Isaiah 53:5)

DON'T SAY: I will never make it through this test.

Say: I can do all things through Christ that strengtheneth me. (Philippians 4:13)

DON'T SAY: I'm too (skinny, fat, tall, dark, short, etc.). I will never be accepted.

Say: I'm fearfully and wonderfully made. (Psalms 139:14)

Don't say: I don't know where our next meal is going to come from.
Say: Yet I've not seen the righteous forsaken nor his seed begging bread. (Psalm 37:25)

Don't say: Giving to others is not important.
Say: Give and it shall be given unto you, good measure, pressed down and shaken together running over shall men give unto your bosom. (Luke 6:38).

Don't say: I'm worried that it's not going to work out right.
Say: Thou will Keep him in perfect peace, whose mind is stayed on thee because he trusteth in thee. (Isaiah 26:3)

Don't say: It's not God's will for me to prosper.
Say: Beloved, I wish above all things that thou mayest prosper and be in health even as thy soul prospereth. (3 John 1:2)

Don't say: My children will never be successful.
Say: The fruit of my womb is blessed. (Deuteronomy 7:13)

Don't say: I'll never get a promotion.
Say: For promotion cometh neither from the east, nor

the west nor from the south but God is the judge; he putteth down one and setteth up another. (Psalms 75:6-7)

DON'T SAY: I'll handle this matter on my own.

Say: For the Lord is our defense; and the Holy One of Israel is our King. (Psalms 89:18)

JESUS SAID it this way in Matthew 12:35-37, "A good man out of the good treasure of the heart bringeth forth good things: and an evil man out of the evil treasure bringeth forth evil things. But I say unto you, That every idle word that men shall speak, they shall give account thereof in the day of judgment. For by thy words thou shalt be justified, and by thy words thou shalt be condemned."

The Message translations reads, "Every one of these careless words is going to come back to haunt you. There will be a time of Reckoning. Words are powerful; take them seriously. Words can be your salvation. Words can also be your damnation." (Matthew 12:36-37 MSG)

Here are more scriptures highlighting the importance of your words.

For verily I say unto you, That whosoever shall say unto this mountain, Be thou removed, and be thou cast into the sea; and shall not doubt in his heart, but shall believe that those things which he saith shall come to pass; he shall have whatsoever he saith. Therefore I say unto you, What things soever ye desire, when ye pray, believe that ye receive them, and ye shall have them. And when ye stand praying, forgive, if ye have ought against any: that your Father also which is in heaven may forgive you your trespasses. But if ye do not forgive, neither will your Father which is in heaven forgive your trespasses. Mark 11:23-26

DEATH AND LIFE are in the power of the tongue: and they that love it shall eat the fruit thereof. Proverbs 18:21

THOU SHALT ALSO DECREE A THING, and it shall be established unto thee: and the light shall shine upon thy ways. Job 22:28

OUR WORDS HAVE SO much power. We must be careful how we speak. As a representative of the Kingdom of God, we have been given authority over the earth. And often, because of what we don't know, we use words very loosely. Hopefully, by now, you have an understanding of how powerful your words are, and you will begin to think before you speak. This is a principle that unfortunately, we have had to learn the hard way because "loose lips sink ships".

Another practical example of this is how, oftentimes, we have out of ignorance spoken negative words over our children. Phrases like, "You just always have to act up, do you?" or "You've got a lot of book sense but no common sense," and "You're turning out to be just like [somebody else]," can become lodged in a child's heart.

But we thank God that He's given us the grace and understanding to correct things that we have spoken and reverse the effects of what we have spoken by replacing it with what God says about our children. If you have spoken negative words over yourself or your children, repent. Say out loud, "I cast down every negative word spoken over myself and my children," and start to speak only the words in the Bible that God says about children.

Beloved, God's word says that we are kings and priests

and that we are created in HIS image. God used words to create everything that exists, and because we are children of God, we have that same creative ability. When we decree a thing, or speak words, what we say shall come to pass. This is another reason why we must be careful to only speak life and not death over our circumstances. The word of God says "Thou shalt decree a thing and it shall be established unto thee: and a light shall shine upon thy ways" (Job 22:28).

DROUGHT INTERRUPTER #4: Kingdom Authority

WE HAVE THE AUTHORITY, like Adam, as Kingdom Ambassadors and Kingdom Citizens. If you want to know God's original intent for mankind, again you must start from the book of beginnings (Genesis). In Genesis 1:26, we find God's original intent for his children. It reads, "And God said, Let us make man in our image, after our likeness; and let them have dominion (authority) over the fish of the sea, and over the fowl of the air, and over the cattle, and over all the earth, and over every creeping thing that creepeth upon the earth." There we see that from the very beginning, we were given Kingdom authority. It is our responsibility to use that authority. And we should not allow the enemy to use our authority against us. We are representing our Father as Ambassadors in the earth and because of who we represent, there is a certain confidence that we should have simply because of who our Father is.

Meditate on these scriptures to gain an understanding of who has the higher power:

Then he called his twelve disciples together, and gave them power and authority over all devils, and to cure diseases. And he sent them to preach the kingdom of God and to heal the sick. Luke 9:1-2

And the seventy returned again with joy, saying, Lord, even the devils are subject unto us through thy name. And he said unto them, I beheld Satan as lightning fall from heaven. Vs 19 Behold, I give unto you power to tread on serpents and scorpions, and over all the power of the enemy: and nothing shall by any means hurt you. Luke 10:17-19

Drought Interrupter #5 - Kingdom Giving

EVERYTHING STARTS WITH A SEED. There is a difference between how the children of light handle money and how the children of darkness handle money. For example, the world's way of acquiring wealth is to save. But as a child of the kingdom of light, you give. This is a spiritual law, just like the law of gravity. If you were to jump off of a building, the law of gravity dictates you are going to plummet down to the earth.

Well, the same spiritual principle applies in the area of giving. If you obey God in the area of giving, whatever you sow, that shall you also reap. *Be not deceived God is not mocked; for whatsoever a man soweth, that shall he also reap.* (Galatians 6:7)

Is it possible that the drought-like conditions you are experiencing in life today are not the devil but a result of something you have sowed in your life unknowingly? Perhaps you're wondering why you don't have any friends? Yet, you are guarded and have a tendency to not allow anyone to get close to you. That could be the seed that you have sown. In Proverbs 18:24, we learn, "A man that hath friends must shew himself friendly and there is a friend that sticketh closer than a brother." Therefore giving and receiving applies not only in the area of finances. You reap what you sow. If you feel you have sown negatively, ask God to forgive you, and sow positive seed going forward. Although, we cannot always prevent the negative harvest that is going to come forth, we can ask for mercy and I do believe the Lord will give you the grace to endure.

Below are a few related scriptures, that I believe will help you to further understand the principles regarding giving.

WHILE THE EARTH REMAINETH, seedtime and harvest, and cold and heat, and summer and winter, and day and night shall not cease. Genesis 8:22

FOR GOD so loved the world, that he gave his only begotten Son, that whosoever believeth in him should not perish, but have everlasting life. John 3:16

GIVE, and it shall be given unto you; good measure, pressed down, and shaken together, and running over, shall men give into your bosom. For with the same measure that ye mete withal it shall be measured to you again. Luke 6:38

A MAN'S gift maketh room for him, and bringeth him before great men. Proverbs 18:16

THIS CAN ALSO MEAN your financial gift! For instance, the Lord puts on your heart to sow a significant seed, and you obey God. I've seen instances where, because of sacrificial giving, doors open that otherwise would remain closed.

DROUGHT INTERRUPTER #6 - Kingdom Wisdom

THE WORD of God states in James 1:5, "If any of you lack wisdom, let him ask of God, that giveth to all men liberally, and upbraideth not; and it shall be given him. But let him ask in faith, nothing wavering. For he that wavereth is like a wave of the sea driven with the wind and tossed. For let not that man think that he shall receive any thing of the Lord. A double minded man is unstable in all his ways."

This passage of Scripture brings me to the next Drought Interrupter, and that's wisdom. We learn in Proverbs 4:7, "Wisdom is the principal thing; therefore get wisdom: and with all thy getting get understanding. Exalt her, and she shall promote thee: she shall bring thee to honour, when thou dost embrace her. She shall give to thine head an ornament of grace: a crown of glory shall she deliver to thee."

Friends, over the years, I made tons of foolish decisions. And it wasn't until I sought the Lord for wisdom did things begin to turnaround. I remember dealing with a problem on my job. I knew that if I handled it on my own way, it would result in the situation getting worse. So I asked God for wisdom in how to deal with the problem. Now understand, wisdom is knowing what to do when you don't know what to do. When I asked the Lord, He answered. He gave me wisdom and everything worked out for my good and His glory.

Also I'm reminded of King Solomon, the richest man who ever lived. He didn't become rich because he asked God for money. No, he became rich because he asked God for wisdom. King Solomon knew when he was crowned King of Israel that without God's wisdom, he wouldn't succeed as King.

In Gibeon, the Lord appeared to Solomon in a dream by night. "And God said, Ask what I shall give thee. And Solomon said, Thou hast shewed unto thy servant David my father great mercy, according as he walked before thee in truth, and in righteousness, and in uprightness of heart with thee; and thou hast kept for him this great kindness, that thou hast given him a son to sit on his throne, as it is this day. And now, O Lord my God, thou hast made thy servant king instead of David my father: and I am but a little child: I know not how to go out or come in. And thy servant is in the midst of thy people which thou hast chosen, a great people, that cannot be numbered nor counted for multitude. Give therefore thy servant an understanding heart to judge thy people, that I may discern between good and bad: for who is able to judge this thy so great a people? And the speech pleased the Lord, that Solomon had asked this thing. And God said unto him, Because thou hast asked this thing, and hast not asked for thyself long life; neither hast asked riches for thyself, nor hast asked the life of thine enemies; but hast asked for thyself understanding to discern judgment; Behold, I have done according to thy words: lo, I have given thee a wise and an understanding heart; so that there was none like thee before thee, neither after thee shall any arise like unto thee. And I have also given thee that which thou hast not asked, both riches, and honour: so that there shall not be any among the kings like unto thee all thy days. (1 Kings 3:5-13)

The Lord not only blessed Solomon with the wisdom that he asked for to lead the children of Israel, but He also blessed him with riches and honor. Because of these blessings, King Solomon was known as the wisest man who ever lived. Solomon, had to first go to God and acknowledge that he had a drought in the area of wisdom and I believe because of his willingness to seek God for wisdom and not riches, God exceeded what he asked for. Furthermore, this lets me know that God's wisdom is critically important to interrupting a drought in one's life.

I have listed Scriptures below to meditate upon regarding the importance of operating in Gods wisdom:

AND UNTO MAN HE SAID, Behold, the fear of the Lord, that is wisdom; and to depart from evil is understanding. Job 28:28

O LORD, how manifold are thy works! in wisdom hast thou made them all: the earth is full of thy riches. Psalms 104:24

The fear of the Lord is the beginning of knowledge: but fools despise wisdom and instruction. Proverbs 1:7

AND JOSHUA the son of Nun was full of the spirit of wisdom; for Moses had laid his hands upon him: and the children of Israel hearkened unto him, and did as the Lord commanded Moses. Deuteronomy 34:9

AND JESUS INCREASED in wisdom and stature, and in favour with God and man. Luke 2:52

DROUGHT INTERRUPTER #7 - **Kingdom Filled Praise**

I BELIEVE with my whole heart that when you praise the Lord, you set the atmosphere to receive change in your situation, deliverance from any unclean forces of darkness, and healing in your body. We also need to understand that when we praise God, it should not be because of what HE does for us, but instead because of who HE is. However, oftentimes, we do things out of routine. And I'm a firm believer that when you praise God, you enter into a realm of the spirit reserved for HIS children.

Consider these scriptures as you open your mouth in praise:

BUT THOU ART HOLY, O thou that inhabitest the praises of Israel. Psalm 22:3

THOU WILT SHEW me the path of life: in thy presence is fulness of joy; at thy right hand, there are pleasures for evermore. Psalms 16:11.

PRAISE YE THE LORD.
Praise God in his sanctuary:
praise him in the firmament of his power.
Praise him for his mighty acts:

praise him according to his excellent greatness.
Praise him with the sound of the trumpet:
praise him with the psaltery and harp.
Praise him with the timbrel and dance:
praise him with stringed instruments and organs.
Praise him upon the loud cymbals:
praise him upon the high sounding cymbals.
Let every thing that hath breath praise the Lord.
Praise ye the Lord.
Psalms 150:1-6

AND SHE CONCEIVED AGAIN, and bare a son: and she said, Now will I praise the Lord: therefore she called his name Judah; and left bearing. Genesis 29:35

PRAISE YE the Lord for the avenging of Israel, when the people willingly offered themselves. Judges 5:2

AND HE APPOINTED certain of the Levites to minister before the ark of the Lord, and to record, and to thank and praise the Lord God of Israel: I Chronicles 16:4

AND WHEN HE had consulted with the people, he appointed singers unto the Lord, and that should praise the beauty of holiness, as they went out before the army, and to say, Praise the Lord; for his mercy endureth for ever. 2 Chronicles 20:21

I WILL PRAISE THEE, O Lord, with my whole heart;

I will shew forth all thy marvellous works.
I will be glad and rejoice in thee:
I will sing praise to thy name, O thou most High.
When mine enemies are turned back,
they shall fall and perish at thy presence.
For thou hast maintained my right and my cause;
thou satest in the throne judging right.

Thou hast rebuked the heathen, thou hast destroyed the wicked, thou hast put out their name for ever and ever.

Psalms 9:1-5

WHEN YOU PRAISE THE LORD, you are telling HIM what HE means to you. You magnify God over your circumstances! When you are praising God, you are breaking off strongholds in your life. There is a heaviness that is lifted when you open your mouth and praise God. As a child of God, we have a responsibility to give God praise. Things happen in the heavenlies when we give God praise.

6

UNCLEAN SPIRITUAL FORCES

We must be aware that we are not earthly beings having a spiritual experience. Instead, we are spirit beings having an earthly experience. In Genesis 1:26-27, the word of God says, "And God said, Let us make man in our image, after our likeness: and let them have dominion over the fish of the sea, and over the fowl of the air, and over the cattle, and over all the earth, and over every creeping thing that creepeth upon the earth. So God created man in his own image, in the image of God created he him; male and female created he them." We learn in John 4:24 that God is spirit. So if we are made in His image, we are also, at the core, spirit beings. As a spirit being, we were born to rule over the earth—the natural realm and also the spiritual realm.

In scripture it also says, that, "While we look not at the things which are seen, but at the things which are not seen: for the things which are seen are temporal; but the things which are not seen are eternal" 2 Corinthians 4:18. In layman terms, the spiritual realm is more real than the physical realm. If satan had his way, he would have you ignorant of your spiritual identity as well as the fact that God has given us supernatural authority over unclean spiritual forces.

I remember after ministering in Lubbock, Texas at the first 'Drought is Over' conference. We witnessed the Lord moving in a very powerful, supernatural way. When I say signs and wonders follow them that believe, that is exactly what happened! Immediately after the preaching, the testimonies began to pour in from individuals sharing how the Lord changed their lives. I mean, the people in that meeting were literally being delivered and set free from spiritual bondage. And because of it, the enemy was very upset. Now, keep in mind, his primary job is to kill, steal and destroy, but the scripture states that *Jesus came that we may have life, and have it more abundantly.* (John 10:10) The move of God was amazing.

At the end of the meeting, I went back to the hotel. Needless to say, I was exhausted and totally drenched from ministering to the people of God. I went straight to bed. But as I drifted off into a deep sleep, I encountered a supernatural presence like never before. It was an actual demonic spirit that had manifested itself. And all I knew was that I needed help immediately. So, I began to pray. I literally could hear myself crying out, "Jesus! Jesus! The name that is above every name." And I shouted, "Satan the Lord rebuke you!" Immediately, the demonic spirit dissipated. Just like that—it disappeared!

We are informed in Ephesians 6:12, "For we wrestle not against flesh and blood, but against principalities, against powers, against the rulers of the darkness of this world, against spiritual wickedness in high places." When I awoke the next morning, the Lord confirmed that HE, had used me during that meeting the night before, and had indeed wrought havoc on the kingdom of darkness in that region. The enemy was upset. But it didn't matter, because, greater is HE that is in me, then he that is in the world.

I thank God that HE prepared me ahead of time by leading me to pray and fast prior to the meeting, which prepared me spiritually for what I would encounter that night. And I believe that had I been in a drought in my spiritual life, I wouldn't have been victorious in the encounter. Always remember that preparation is NEVER time wasted.

I would like to encourage you as a believer in Christ, that as the Lord prompts you, to always try to be obedient to His voice. It could be something as simple as praying for a particular person who comes to mind or maybe even sowing a sacrificial seed in a particular ministry even though it may not be in your budget. Beloved, when we follow the leading of the Spirit of God and don't doubt or refuse to obey HIM, the rewards have always far exceeded our expectations.

The word of God is full of promises that will enable you to interrupt the potential drought in your life. But we must do our part. I look at it like a partnership. We have a very important part to play in the purpose and plan God has for our lives. Our part is simply called obedience. We must obey his word if we expect to see the manifestation of HIS promises in our lives.

In the previous chapters, I have shared many scriptures that prove God's word is true. And in addition, I would like to encourage you with this one in Isaiah 44:3. *For I will pour water upon him that is thirsty, and floods upon the dry ground; I will pour my spirit upon thy seed l and my blessing upon thine offspring.*

7

KINGDOM FORGIVENESS

I believe the key of forgiveness is so very critical when it comes to interrupting the drought in your life. Oftentimes, believe it or not, unforgiveness will block a release of God's promises in your life. I heard it stated this way, "It's like you drinking poison but hoping your enemy dies." It sounds ridiculous, doesn't it? But it's true. You would be surprised of the number of individuals that are praying religiously and are not seeing the answers to their prayers manifested in their lives. And they are scratching their heads and asking, "why"? Well, the purpose of this key is to expose the enemy's tactics so that you can begin to see the drought interrupted in your life. This key is so important that it gets a chapter all of its own.

Implementing this key begins by forgiving the individual(s) that hurt you. This doesn't mean you allow them to hurt you again, but that you release them from the debt they owe you. There was a situation in my life where I was treated very badly and unfairly by an old supervisor and a root of bitterness began to grow in my heart. I knew my supervisor was being used by the enemy. This unfair treatment lasted for several months, but it was not until I began to pray for this individual and see them as God saw them that I began to see a difference in my heart. I had to walk by faith in God's word and let the bitterness GO!

It was easier said than done. However, I knew the decision to forgive could not be based on my feelings. The conscious decision would have to be based on my obedience to God's word. When I yielded to His word, God softened my heart and things changed dramatically. This person began to open up about the problems they were having with one of their family members and their whole attitude changed towards me. I was able to understand their treatment of me had absolutely nothing to do with me. This individual was only manifesting a far deeper issue that was going on in their personal life. It had nothing to do with me except to serve as a God-ordained opportunity to grow in love.

Studies have found that unforgiveness is often the source of internal health issues like stress, cancer and other illnesses. Case studies show that when a person harbors unforgiveness in their heart, it can manifest in critical and long-term illness[i]. So, beloved, understand that forgiveness is more for you than the other person. And because the word of God says we are to forgive, we need to trust that the Lord will never steer us wrong.

Medical science confirms the importance of forgiveness.

"There is an enormous physical burden to being hurt and disappointed," says Karen Swartz, M.D., director of the Mood Disorders Adult Consultation Clinic at The Johns Hopkins Hospital. Chronic anger puts you into a fight-or-flight mode, which results in numerous changes in heart rate, blood pressure and immune response. Those changes then increase the risk of depression, heart disease and diabetes, among other conditions. Forgiveness, however, calms stress levels, leading to improved health.[1]

Recognize that it often takes a supernatural enablement from the Lord to forgive. I will go so far as to say that it is almost impossible to forgive some things without a supernatural endowment. But that is good news because we *are* supernatural in Christ! We are filled with true love in our hearts by the Holy Spirit (Romans 5:5), and forgiveness is at the core of God's love.

Here are scriptures you can meditate on regarding the importance of forgiving someone who may have hurt or disappointed you.

YE HAVE HEARD that it hath been said, An eye for an eye, and a tooth for a tooth: But I say unto you, That ye resist not evil: but whosoever shall smite thee on thy right cheek, turn to him the other also. And if any man will sue thee at the law, and take away thy coat, let him have thy cloke also. And whosoever shall compel thee to go a mile, go with him twain. Give to him that asketh thee, and from him that would borrow of thee turn not thou away. Matthew 5:39-44

AFTER THIS MANNER therefore pray ye: Our Father which art in heaven, Hallowed be thy name. Thy kingdom come. Thy will be done in earth, as it is in heaven. Give us this day our daily bread. And forgive us our debts, as we forgive our debtors. And lead us not into temptation, but deliver us from evil: For thine is the kingdom, and the power, and the glory, for ever. Amen. For if ye forgive men their trespasses, your heavenly Father will also forgive you: But if ye forgive not men their trespasses, neither will your Father forgive your trespasses. Mathew 6:12-16

Then came Peter to him, and said, Lord, how oft shall my brother sin against me, and I forgive him? till seven times? Jesus saith unto him, I say not unto thee, Until seven times: but, Until seventy times seven. Matthew 18:18-25

Therefore I say unto you, What things soever ye desire, when ye pray, believe that ye receive them, and ye shall have them. And when ye stand praying, forgive, if ye have ought against any: that your Father also which is in heaven may forgive you your trespasses. But if ye do not forgive, neither will your Father which is in heaven forgive your trespasses. Mark 11:24-26

But I say unto you which hear, Love your enemies, do good to them which hate you, Bless them that curse you, and pray for them which despitefully use you. And unto him that smiteth thee on the one cheek offer also the other; and him that taketh away thy cloke forbid not to take thy coat also. Luke 6:27-29

Take heed to yourselves: If thy brother trespass against thee, rebuke him; and if he repent, forgive him. And if he trespass against thee seven times in a day, and seven times in a day turn again to thee, saying, I repent; thou shalt forgive him. Luke 17:3-4

Bless them which persecute you: bless, and curse not. Rejoice with them that do rejoice, and weep with them that weep. Be of the same mind one toward another. Mind not high things, but condescend to men of low estate. Be not wise in your own conceits.

Recompense to no man evil for evil. Provide things honest in the sight of all men. If it be possible, as much as lieth in you, live peaceably with all men. Dearly beloved, avenge not yourselves, but rather give place unto wrath: for it is written, Vengeance is mine; I will repay, saith the Lord. Therefore if thine enemy hunger, feed him; if he thirst, give him drink: for in so doing thou shalt heap coals of fire on his head. Be not overcome of evil, but overcome evil with good. Romans 12:14-21

LET ALL BITTERNESS, *and wrath, and anger, and clamour, and evil speaking, be put away from you, with all malice: And be ye kind one to another, tenderhearted, forgiving one another, even as God for Christ's sake hath forgiven you.* Ephesians 4:31-32

PUT ON THEREFORE, *as the elect of God, holy and beloved, bowels of mercies, kindness, humbleness of mind, meekness, longsuffering; Forbearing one another, and forgiving one another, if any man have a quarrel against any: even as Christ forgave you, so also do ye. And above all these things put on charity, which is the bond of perfectness. And let the peace of God rule in your hearts, to the which also ye are called in one body; and be ye thankful.* Colossians 3:12-15

HERE IS a short list of examples in the Bible where forgiveness was demonstrated:
Esau forgives Jacob (Genesis 33:4)
Joseph forgives his brothers (Gen 45:1-15)
Moses forgives the Israelites (Numbers 12:1-13)
David forgives Saul (1 Samuel 24:10-12)
Solomon forgives Adonjah (1 King 1:50-53)

Jesus forgives his enemies (Luke 23:34)

PRAYERFULLY, these scriptures and examples will provide a road map for you to find it in your heart to move forward toward your journey to freedom in the area of forgiveness, so that you may enjoy a life full of God's promises for your life as you conquer another drought interrupter. Remember, it's only through a sincere relationship with our Heavenly Father and our Lord Jesus Christ that we can find it in our hearts to forgive as Christ has forgiven us.

8

KINGDOM FILLED REPENTANCE

From that time Jesus began to preach, and to say, Repent: for the kingdom of heaven is at hand. (Mark 4:17)

From this scripture, we know repentance is something we should all do. Why? Because Jesus said SO. But what does it actually mean to repent? The word "repent" means: a change of mind that results in a change of action, which would mean you are no longer practicing the act of disobedience towards God.

Oftentimes the enemy will deceive us into thinking that because we are under the dispensation of grace, God will understand. We use the old familiar phrase, "I'm only human," as an excuse to stay in sin. Well, that's a bunch of hogwash. If it's in the Bible, and God's word tells us we should abstain from sin, I firmly believe that HE will give us the grace to obey HIS word concerning it. Furthermore, for a believer, the phrase "I'm only human" is not true. You are actually a new creation (a new species) in Christ (2 Corinthians 5:17). Non-believing humans do not have the power of the Holy Spirit living in them. You, however, do!

For example, as a single woman, I know that we as

Kingdom believers should not participate in sex outside of marriage. We should be abstinent. Well, what's troubling to me is the alarming number of individuals who say they are blood-washed, tongue-talking believers; yet, they think it's okay to engage in sex before marriage. That's a trick of the enemy! I am one among many believers who are living a celibate lifestyle.

You may be asking how this is possible in this day and age. Well, I'm glad you asked. In today's culture it seems as though everyone is sexually active. When the discussion arises regarding the subject of intimacy outside of marriage, I've even been called "old fashioned". Well, call me old fashioned! But I disagree. It's not old fashioned, it's merely obeying God's word.

As I said earlier, if God says it in HIS word, that we should abstain from sex before marriage, (and HE does!), then I believe He will give us the grace to abstain. But we have to do our part by not making any provisions for the flesh.

For an example, if you are actively dating someone, don't allow that individual to come to your house, especially when you know there is a clear attraction to one another. Instead, when you both go on a date, make it clear up front, plan to meet each other at the location and at the end of the date, you both go your separate ways. I'm telling you, it works. I know from experience. But if for some reason you do fall, it is imperative that you repent immediately. Don't keep repeating the same thing over and over again. Don't waste the grace!

Below are scriptures and examples pertaining to repentance.

If so be they will hearken, and turn every man from his evil way, that I may repent me of the evil, which I purpose to do unto them because of the evil of their doings. And thou shalt say unto them, Thus saith the Lord; If ye will not hearken to me, to walk in my law, which I have set before you, To hearken to the words of my servants the prophets, whom I sent unto you, both rising up early, and sending them, but ye have not hearkened; Then will I make this house like Shiloh, and will make this city a curse to all the nations of the earth. So the priests and the prophets and all the people heard Jeremiah speaking these words in the house of the Lord. Jeremiah 26:3-6

I ACKNOWLEDGED my sin unto thee,
 and mine iniquity have I not hid.
 I said, I will confess my transgressions unto the Lord;
 and thou forgavest the iniquity of my sin. Selah.
 Psalm 32:5

DEPART FROM EVIL, and do good;
 seek peace, and pursue it.
 Psalm 34:14

HE THAT COVERETH his sins shall not prosper:
 but whoso confesseth and forsaketh them shall have mercy. Proverbs 28:13

AND GOD SAW THEIR WORKS, that they turned from their evil way; and God repented of the evil, that he had said that he would do unto them; and he did it not. Jonah 3:10

COME, and let us return unto the Lord:
>*for he hath torn, and he will heal us;*
>*he hath smitten, and he will bind us up.*
>*After two days will he revive us:*
>*in the third day he will raise us up,*
>*and we shall live in his sight.*
>*Then shall we know, if we follow on to know the Lord:*
>*his going forth is prepared as the morning;*
>*and he shall come unto us as the rain,*
>*as the latter and former rain unto the earth.*
>Hosea 6:1-3

FOR GODLY SORROW worketh repentance to salvation not to be repented of: but the sorrow of the world worketh death. 2 Corinthians 7:10

So, as you can see from these many examples, repentance is not optional. We, as believers, can repent as a way to behave in a manner that is pleasing unto God. We can only do it by God's grace.

9

KINGDOM DELIVERANCE

The enemy is behind the scenes. For some of the situations we encounter as believers, we will require the ministry of deliverance to break the stronghold in our lives. Perhaps you have noticed a pattern in your family; a stubborn, continued negative cycle of dysfunction. And no matter what you do, it's as though history keeps repeating itself over and over again. Examples include a family history of children being birthed out of wedlock, generation after generation of alcoholics, poverty, imprisonment, and/or mental instability. Perhaps you pray continually for your loved ones. You may even go on a 21-day fast, but nothing seems to be working for long. Then you get frustrated with the whole matter and begin to reason, "Maybe this is how things are supposed to be." Well, what you are seeing is the manifestation of a drought in your family or maybe even a generational curse. This is not the way it's supposed to be, for God's will is for everyone to be set free.

Every curse in a believer's life can be broken. It's important for you to break it at the point of entry into your family's bloodline because such specific, persistent curses are the result of a door left open that you are not aware of. What do I mean by an open door? It is a point in history where someone in your family made an allegiance with the enemy, and the enemy loves to enforce the law when it's in his favor. Could it be possible that one of your forefathers made an oath with the Free Masons or became involved in the occult? Little did they know, those choices opened doors to demonic activity in your family's bloodline. And oftentimes, it's what we don't know that the enemy uses against the body of Christ. You know this already, because just like sin entered all mankind through Adam's bloodline, so can other permissions be granted that pass down from generation to generation.

Fear itself can open a door to a generational curse in your life. As a child you may have witnessed someone drown, and now you have a fear of water. We must understand that *God hath not given us the spirit of fear, but of power love and a sound mind.* (2 Timothy 1:7).

The good news is that just like sin entered through one man's actions, freedom comes through Jesus (1 Corinthians 15:21). Jesus declared in Luke 4:18, "The Spirit of the Lord is upon me, because he hath anointed me to preach the gospel to the poor; he hath sent me to heal the brokenhearted, to preach deliverance to the captives, and recovering of sight to the blind, to set at liberty them that are bruised." Beloved, I have great news! Jesus died that we may be set free and delivered in every area of our lives. We need to understand that in Jesus' ministry, He healed the sick, saved the lost and cast out demons.

But unfortunately, in this generation, we don't see a lot of deliverance ministry going forth. Which means, many people in the body of Christ are saved, yet bound because they have not enforced their own freedom. It's like when someone opens a bird's cage, but the bird refuses to fly out.

Now, please understand, that in Christ, a believer cannot be demon possessed. However, you can be harassed by a demon and be influenced by spiritual wickedness in high places. You will still go to heaven, but will continue to struggle with depression, poverty, alcohol and such if you choose to stay in the cage throughout this life. That should not be so.

As I look back over my life, there was a history of broken relationships and I didn't understand why. The people in my family just always seemed to get disconnected from one another somehow. And it wasn't until much later in my walk with Christ that I began to understand the abundant life that Jesus came to give us applied to my family relationships as well. But to experience life abundantly, we must do things according to God's way. If we lean to the same understanding the generations before us leaned on, we will not see God's best. After all, it was the generational patterns of thinking and acting that got us messed up in the first place.

Understanding this pattern, my friend, began my journey of seeking God for HIS way of maintaining family relationships. Matthew 5:6 declares, "Blessed are they which do hunger and thirst after righteousness: for they shall be filled." I believed God's word and took hold of the promise that the Lord Himself would reveal to me HIS plan for breakthrough and deliverance for myself and the generations to follow.

The process for deliverance consists of five (5) simple but powerful steps.

1. Acknowledge that you're in need of deliverance.
2. Repent and renounce any involvement in the

occult or any activity that you know is contrary to the will of God.
3. Forgive anyone who has wronged you.
4. Take your stand on God's word.
5. Expel. And to expel means to breath out. Exhale. And receive your deliverance by Faith, in Jesus' Name.

You are free in Christ! Come out of that cage!

10

KINGDOM LOVE

The power of love is the rod by which ALL of the Drought Interrupters hang. In other words, nothing in the Kingdom of God will work without love. *Though I speak with the tongues of men and of angels, and have not charity, I am become as sounding brass, or a tinkling cymbal. And though I have the gift of prophecy, and understand all mysteries, and all knowledge; and though I have all faith, so that I could remove mountains, and have not charity, I am nothing. And though I bestow all my goods to feed the poor, and though I give my body to be burned, and have not charity, it profiteth me nothing.*

Charity suffereth long, and is kind; charity envieth not; charity vaunteth not itself, is not puffed up, Doth not behave itself unseemly, seeketh not her own, is not easily provoked, thinketh no evil; Rejoiceth not in iniquity, but rejoiceth in the truth; Beareth all things, believeth all things, hopeth all things, endureth all things.

Charity never faileth: but whether there be prophecies, they shall fail; whether there be tongues, they shall cease; whether there be knowledge, it shall vanish away. For we know in part, and we prophesy in part. But when that which is perfect is come, then that which is in part shall be done away.

When I was a child, I spake as a child, I understood as a child, I thought as a child: but when I became a man, I put away childish things. For now we see through a glass, darkly; but then face to face: now I know in part; but then shall I know even as also I am known.

And now abideth faith, hope, charity, these three; but the greatest of these is charity. (1 Corinthians 12:1-13)

This scripture is telling us that you can be the most gifted person in the world, but if you don't show love to your fellow brother or sister, your giftedness means nothing.

The love walk can only be demonstrated through the grace granted to us by the death, burial and resurrection of Jesus Christ. There are countless testimonies of individuals who have experienced extreme hardships, yet found it in their hearts to love because we as believers are commanded to love. The real love of Christ is unconditional. In other words, it doesn't keep score of any wrongdoing. And it certainly doesn't keep bringing up the wrong that you may have done. Again, these are Drought Interrupters that are sure to release a gully-washing, downpour of rain in your life and illuminate potential drought.

Jesus was the first one to demonstrate unconditional love. John 3:16 states, "For God so loved the world, that he gave his only begotten Son, that whosoever believeth in him should not perish, but have everlasting life." He so loved us.

You may be thinking, "Well of course Jesus can love unconditionally. He's God. But it's difficult to love someone who abused me, or left me for another man or woman." Well, you're right. It is difficult, but not impossible. You must love from the inside out. It must come from the heart, and it's not always easy.

There are three types of love: phileo, eros and agape. The love I'm describing is agape. This love is a total love, which can only come from a loving God!

The word of God reads in Mark 12:28-31, "And one of the scribes came, and having heard them reasoning together, and perceiving that he had answered them well, asked him, Which is the first commandment of all? And Jesus answered him, The first of all the commandments is, Hear, O Israel; The Lord our God is one Lord: And thou shalt love the Lord thy God with all thy heart, and with all thy soul, and with all thy mind, and with all thy strength: this is the first commandment. And the second is like, namely this, Thou shalt love thy neighbor as thyself. There is none other commandment greater than these."

I conclude that we have the ultimate example of love in that of the unconditional, sacrificial love Jesus gave for the world. Jesus is our example of true love. And as we strive daily to be like HIM, I believe it is possible to love one day at a time, with the ultimate desire to obtain the complete and uncontaminated love that HE shows us every day.

Matthew 5:43-48 lets us know that our love should extend beyond those who are lovable and those who treat us well. Loving nice, easy-to-get-along-with people is not a measure of our love. How we feel about and treat those who mistreat us is the true gauge.

A FINAL NOTE

Beloved, there you have it. *Drought Interrupters*. If you cultivate them, they are sure to interrupt the drought in your life. Although this collection is by no means exhaustive, I can say that what I have shared are a few Kingdom keys that are sure to release a consistent flow of God's promises in every area of your life, if you chose to operate in them.

Prophetic declaration:

Father, in the name of Jesus, I decree and declare a supernatural release of every dry place in this reader's life. I thank you, Lord, that as they read this book, every negative cycle in their life has been broken. Every generational curse has been reversed! And their life will never be the same again! I thank You that Your promises for their life are yea and amen. And from this day forward, I decree and declare that THE DROUGHT IS OVER!!!! In Jesus' NAME, AMEN!!

A PRAYER TO RECEIVE CHRIST AS LORD AND SAVIOR

Romans 10:9-10 says, "That if thou shalt confess with thy mouth the Lord Jesus, and shalt believe in thine heart that God hath raised him from the dead, thou shalt be saved. For with the heart man believeth unto righteousness; and with the mouth confession is made unto salvation." If you believe these words, pray this prayer.

Father, I know that I am a sinner. And I believe Jesus is the son of God, and that He died on the cross for all of my sins. Also, I believe that on the third day He rose from the dead with all power. Jesus, I repent of my sins and I ask You to forgive me of all of my sins. I ask You to come into my heart as my personal Savior and live Your life in and through me. Father, fill me with the Holy Spirit and power and I will live for You. Thank You, Jesus, that I am saved and now I live with You eternally and my name is written in the Lamb's book of life. In Jesus's Name Amen!

Name _____

Date _____

REFERENCES

1. https://www.bcm.edu/news/sports-medicine/thirsty-you-are-already-dehydrated

2. bodybuilder.com

3. Leaf, Caroline. Who Switched Off My Brain?: Controlling Toxic Thoughts and Emotions. N.p.: Inprov, 2009. Print.

4. http://www.hopkinsmedicine.org/health/healthy_aging/healthy_connections/forgiveness-your-health-depends-on-it

NOTES

www.ingramcontent.com/pod-product-compliance
Lightning Source LLC
Chambersburg PA
CBHW070056120526
44588CB00033B/1662